GENOCIDE OF THOUGHT

Original amharic title መንግሥት፣ ልማት እና መገናኛ ብዙኃን በኢትዮጵያ
(Mass Media and Economic Development)
Book design Edwin Smet
ISBN 978-90-823641-3-2

www.evatasfoundation.com

GENOCIDE OF ~~CENSORSHIP IN ETHIOPIA~~ THOUGHT

BISRAT WOLDEMICHAEL HANDISO

Edited by **Peter de Haan**

EVATAS**FOUNDATION**

Amsterdam 2015

_ Acronyms

AU — African Union

AD — Ana Domino

BC — Before Christ

TPLF — Tigray Peoples Liberation Front

EPLF — Eritrean Peoples' Liberation Front

EPRDF — Ethiopian Peoples' Revolutionary Democratic Front

EPDM — Ethiopian People Democratic Movement

ANDM — Amhara National Democratic Movement

OPDO — Oromo Peoples Democratic Organization

SEPDF — South Ethiopian Peoples' Democratic Front

SEPDM — South Ethiopian Peoples' Democratic Movement

GDP — Gross Domestic Product

GNI — Gross National Income

GNC — Gross national consumption

GNP — Gross national product

GTP — Growth and transformation plan

PM — Prime Minster

SNNPR — South nation, nationalities region

Ha — hectare

ETB — Ethiopian birr (currency)

_ Acknowledgements

Without the support from the *Eva Tas Foundation* this essay would not have been published. Therefore, I thank the Foundation with deep gratitude. A special word of thanks is due to my editor, Peter de Haan, who made sure, that my essay did indeed see the light. Thanks to Chalaches Tadesse for his comments and editing of an earlier draft of this essay. I hope that my essay will contribute to a better understanding of the ways in which the Ethiopian government is clamping down on all the free media, be it newspapers, magazines, or the social media, thereby blocking Ethiopia's population from information that would have helped them in forming a balanced opinion about the consequences of the government's negative attitude towards the free media, and about Ethiopia's economic development. Regarding the opposite of the free media and the free expression of opinion, I quote Argentinian journalist, Adolfo Marcovich, who very rightly observed that: *Censorship is the genocide of thought. It kills ideas through omission, ignorance and fear.*

Nairobi, April 2015

/ TABLE
OF CONTENTS

/ INTRODUCTION

This is a story about Ethiopia and the part played by the mass media in pursuit of Ethiopia's development. Unfortunately, free media cannot play the role they should in promoting Ethiopia's social and economic development, despite the fact that Ethiopia's Constitution includes freedom of the press and freedom of expression.

Why the media cannot play their developmental role is the subject matter of this essay. Before treating this essay's central question, however, first a brief description of Ethiopia.

As it has been written in world history books, as well as proven by concrete remains of ancient civilizations, Ethiopia is among the few countries in the world with a very long history of nation-building which started more than three thousand years. Ethiopia reached the level of statehood during the year 2545 B.C. Ethiopia is the only African country with its own alphabet and calendar. However, Ethiopia has never been able to cherish its long and glorious past as Ethiopia was and still is a land of contradictions and unresolved puzzles.

Based on the 2013 World Bank report, Ethiopia's population is projected to stand currently at over 94.1 million, making it the second most populous country in Africa, and 14th in the world. Ethiopia's capital city, Addis Ababa, has a population of over 4 million citizens. Addis is the economic and diplomatic hub of Africa, hosting continental and international organizations, such as the Africa Union (AU), African Development Bank (ADB), the United Nations Economic Commission for Africa (UNECA), and several foreign embassies. However, Ethiopia has darker stories of its own too. The country suffered from long years of civil war that claimed the lives of thousands.

Amharic is the working language of the federal government and of many regional governments, such as Amhara, the Southern Nations, Nationalities, and Peoples' Regional (SNNPR) governments Beneshangul-Gumuz, Gambella, as well as the City Governments of Addis Ababa and Dire Dawa. Other regions, such as Oromia, Tigray, Somali, Afar, and Hareri use the language of the dominant ethnic group residing in the regions concerned. Throughout Ethiopia there are over 70 local languages spoken by the more than 80 ethnic groups.

Ethiopia is the only African country that defended its sovereignty from foreign aggression, with the exception of two Italian occupations; the last one from 1935 to 1941. Ethiopia supported other African countries to win their independence during the 1960s. Ethiopia is considered to be the cradle of mankind; it is the home of Lucy (locally known as "Denkinesh"), who lived 3.2 million years ago. Yet, Ethiopia still is one of the poorest nations in the world.

Ethiopia was ruled by monarchies, hailing from the Solomonic dynasty, who claimed having divine authority. The formation of the modern Ethiopian state traces back to the late 19th century when Emperor Menelik II united the Southern, South-Western and South-Eastern part of the country under a centralized system of government. Emperor Haileseleassie I was the last absolute monarch of the Solomonic dynasty. The Emperor was deposed in 1974 through a popular revolution.

A military junta (in Amharic known as Dergue – Provisional Military Administrative Council) immediately hijacked the popular revolution, thereby ending the hopes of democracy and freedom. The junta – led by Colonel Mengistu Hailemariam – adopted Marxism-Leninism as the state ideology. He ruled the country with an iron-fist. Then, the Dergue transformed itself into the Workers Party of Ethiopia (being the only vanguard party), it adopted a new Constitution, and in 1987 established Ethiopia as a republic.

For over thirty years, the country was plagued by famines (i.e., especially the ones of 1973 and 1984), and was engulfed in a bitter civil war in the provinces of Eritrea and Tigray. In 1991, the war ended when the Ethiopian Peoples' Revolutionary Democratic Front (EPRDF), a coalition of ethnic-based liberation movements, controlled Addis Ababa. After a four years transition period, EPRDF introduced ethnic federalism which forms a prominent part of a new Constitution adopted in 1995. This new Constitution introduced a multiparty parliamentary system and divided the hitherto centralized state into nine regional states, largely on the basis of ethnicity, as well as two city governments: Addis Ababa and Dire Dawa.

The Constitution also established a bicameral parliament (i.e., the House of Peoples' Representatives and the House of Federation) and granted supreme executive powers to the prime minister; the presidency remained symbolic. The 547-seat House of Peoples' Representatives, composed of the country's nationalities, holds the ultimate sovereign power.

Based on the data from the Central Statistics Agency, 83% of the population lives in rural areas, whereas the remaining 17% lives in cities and towns. Agriculture has been the main source of livelihood and the major contributor to GDP in the country. Orthodox Christianity and Islam are the two major religions. However, Protestantism, Catholicism, and traditional religions also have many followers in the country.

The current EPRDF regime oppresses civil and political rights, and so doing, it – in fact – undermines Ethiopia's economic development and social transformation. After all, unless citizens are allowed to freely participate in development and exercise their rights, it is hard to realize democracy and development. The political-economic system maintains the unequal distribution of resources and wealth. Only few pro-regime people benefit from the national cake, while the majority of Ethiopians remain poor and marginalized.

Despite the constitutional recognized freedom of expression and of the press, the EPRDF regime ruthlessly prosecutes owners of free media enterprises, private media journalists, bloggers, and Opposition politicians, thereby systematically weakening private media, opposition political parties, and professional associations. Most of them have either been harassed, imprisoned, or exiled for merely exercising the right of freedom of expression. Several international human rights organizations, such as Amnesty International and Human Rights Watch, accuse the regime of committing serious human rights violations. In short, the ruling party has effectively grabbed all political and social space, so much so that it has now become a semi-authoritarian regime.

This essay is composed as follows. Chapter One describes the Evolution and Trends in Mass Media since the 1990s. Chapter Two sketches Ethiopia's economic development since the 1990s, while Chapter Three deals with the question whether journalism can play its professional role in Ethiopia's development.

Various annexes provide additional, detailed, information on some of this essay's themes. Annexe I describes the nature and evolution of the Ethiopian state and government. Annexe II includes a detailed overview of the origin of modern mass media in Ethiopia. Annexe III provides a table of large-scale land allocations and rent prices. And finally, Annexe IV includes the basic principles of journalism.

/ CHAPTER ONE

EVOLUTION AND TRENDS IN MASS MEDIA SINCE THE 1990S

Mass media can be defined as a channel by which information is disseminated from a person, people, or institution to another person, people or institution. The mass media is playing a significant role in ameliorating people's lives. The media also has a massive share in terms of knowledge and technology transfer.

Books were the earliest and foremost channels of information dissemination. Current mainstream media are newspapers, magazines, radio, television, and the Internet. In addition, billboards, flyers, and mobile phones are playing a supportive role in disseminating information.

_ 1.1. Objectives of Media

All media share three main principal objectives in terms of information dissemination; i.e., to educate, to inform, and to entertain. In terms of educating the public, the media provides education to the public on social, political, and economic issues with a view to enhance their knowledge and to improve their social and economic position.

Independent media transmit unbiased information, promote human rights, and facilitate the creation of a society with strong democratic institutions. These media serve as *the fourth branch of the state* by providing checks and balances on government's actions, which – in turn – contributes to economic development and a fair distribution of resources.

The existence of media that is free from any pressure/influence has great advantages for a society. Free media play a significant role in controlling the proper and lawful accomplishment of the duties of the legislator, the executive, and the judiciary. In addition, the free media is helpful in building a society's institutions and in accelerating its economic development. However, if a government limits the freedom of the media it curbs the possibilities for checks and balances and paves the way for authoritarian and corrupt regimes.

In the political world the efforts of the free media is more effective than armed struggle to remove dictatorial regimes. This is because the media is more effective in mobilizing people in opposing these regimes in pursuit of democratic government.

A strong democracy can only be established through an intelligent and well-informed society that works towards its common good. Free, strong media is an instrument of social change and economic well-being.

Free means free from any beneficial ties with the ruling party or opposition parties. The activities of the free media must be based on professional ethics and in due consideration of the national interest. Another function of free media is to serve as a voice for dissent, e.g., by exposing the misdeeds of authoritarian regimes.

_ 1.2 Press Freedom and Freedom of Expression

In 1993, the EPRDF government announced freedom of the press, freedom of organizing and freedom of thought through the Press Proclamation 34/93. The 1995 Constitution also provided freedom of the press under Articles 29(3) (a) and (b) which stipulates that "freedom of the press and other mass media and freedom of artistic creativity is guaranteed. In the Constitution freedom of the press is also guaranteed through the prohibition of any form of censorship and the guaranteeing of the right of access to information of public interest to media.

The Freedom of the Mass Media and Access to Information Proclamation 590/2008 Article 4(1) states that censorship is not allowed, i.e., "freedom of the mass media is constitutionally guaranteed. Censorship in any form is prohibited." To a limited extent, these rights were somehow in practice until the 15 May 2005 election.

The Ethiopian Constitution, Article 29(1-2), declares that "everyone has the right to hold opinions without interference", and, "everyone has the right to freedom of expression without any interference", which includes the "freedom to seek, receive, and impart information and ideas of all kinds, regardless of frontiers, either orally, in writing or in print, in the form of art, or through any media of his choice". In addition, Ethiopia ratified the Universal Declaration of Human Rights. Article 19 grants the right and freedom of expression. It stipulates that "everyone has the right to freedom of opinion and expression; this right includes freedom to hold opinions without interference and to seek, receive and impart information and ideas through any media and regardless of frontiers."

Ethiopia has signed the above – and other – universal declarations and conventions concerning the right and freedom of expression and access to information. These declarations are applicable as per Article 9(4) of the Constitution which stipulates that "the universal conventions signed by Ethiopia will be considered as part of the law of the land".

However, there are also restrictions. Take, for example, the 2009 Anti-Terrorism Proclamation, and the proclamation that established the Ethiopian Broadcast Authority, the authority that regulates the media in general. These proclamations have been criticized for contravening the Constitution and the international human rights conventions that Ethiopia had ratified. The Anti-Terrorism Proclamation includes Article 14(1) which states:

To prevent and control a terrorist act the National Intelligence and Security Service may, up on getting court warrant intercept or conduct surveillance on the telephone, fax, radio, internet, electronic, postal and similar communications of a person suspected of terrorism; enter into any premise in secrete to enforce the interception; or install or remove instruments enabling the interception.

This article contradicts the Constitution's article 26(2) which states that "everyone has the right to the inviolability of his notes and correspondence including postal letters, and communications made by means of telephone, telecommunications and electronic devices." Nonetheless, Article 14(1) forces journalists and political and human rights activists to conduct strict self-censorship. The Anti-Terrorism Proclamation allows the government to target individuals, institutions, and associations which they consider a threat to their political power, as well as to put society under the wrath of fear. Unfortunately, the rights and freedoms of the press are not practiced in Ethiopia. If they were, there would not have been arrests and mass prosecution of free media, including journalists, bloggers, and leaders of the Opposition. In particular the Anti-Terrorism Proclamation seems to be designed to consolidate the power of the ruling party by silencing the free media.

_ 1.3 Media Crackdown

In a wave of press crackdown in mid-2014, i.e., before the May 2015 general parliamentary elections, the government imprisoned four journalists charged with terrorism offences: Tesfalem Woldeyes, Asmamaw Hailegiorgis, Edom Kassaye, Temesgen Dessalegn, as well as six bloggers from the so-called "Zone-9 Bloggers": Befkadu Hailu, Nathnael Feleke, Atnaf Birhane, Mahlet Fantahun, Abel Wabela, and Zelalem Kibret. One of the co-founders of the *Zone-9 Blog*, Soleyana Shimeles, who is in exile, was also charged with terrorism offence in abstentia.

In August 2014, the Ministry of Justice charged five magazines, one newspaper, and three large circulation magazines namely *Addis Guday*, *Fact* and *Lomi*. Their publishers were eventually sentenced for more than three years.

Prominent journalists who were imprisoned before 2014 include Eskindir Nega (see box below), Woubshet Taye, Reeyot Alemu, Yousuf Getachew and Solomon Kebede. In addition, the government used the Anti-Terrorism Proclamation to charge the exiled journalists of the former "Addis Neger" newspaper – Abey Teklemariam and Mesfin Negash. They were sentenced to eight years of imprisonment in absentia. Eritrean journalists Tesfalidet Kidane and Saleh Idris, as well as Mohammed Aweys from Somalia are also sentenced and imprisoned by the Ethiopian government. Well-known non-violence young politicians such as Andualem Aragie, religious leaders, Ethiopian Muslim Community Representative Committee leaders, some monks of the Ethiopian Orthodix Tewahedo Church (i.e., from Waledeba Monastry), and priests from Tigray are also victims of the Anti-Terrorism Proclamation. The prosecutors used the victims' written documents in their charges.

As editor of the newspaper *Satenaw*, Eskinder Nega was arrested on 28 November 2005 following demonstrations against the results of the Ethiopian general election on 15 May 2005, which saw Meles stay in power but were alleged to be fraudulent. Eskinder was charged with the capital offenses of treason, "outrages against the Constitution" and "incitement to armed conspiracy". Amnesty International (AI) designated him a prisoner of conscience, "detained solely for exercising his right to freedom of expression", and called for his immediate release. AI also protested the "poor and unsanitary" conditions of his detention at Kerchele prison.[1]

Eskinder was found guilty and served seventeen months' imprisonment before being released by presidential pardon at the end of 2007. Eskinder's wife, journalist Serkalem Fasil, was also detained for seventeen months, giving birth to their son Nafkot while still imprisoned. Following the conviction, Eskinder lost his license to practice journalism, and his newspaper was closed by the authorities in 2007. He nonetheless continued to publish online.

Even before 2005, Eskinder was found guilty of terrorism charges on 23 January 2012. As of May 2012 he was awaiting sentencing. At the time, Eskinder's trial drew international attention, with twenty IPI World Press Freedom Heroes co-signing a letter to Meles on 23 April, stating their "extremely strong condemnation of the Ethiopian government's decision to jail journalist Eskinder Nega". The U.S.-based Committee to Protect Journalists (CPJ) described the trial as "an affront to justice" and the accusations as "politicized charges used by the government to intimidate journalists and chill news-gathering activities". Human Rights Watch called on the Ethiopian government to release Eskinder and the imprisoned journalists, stating, "The detention of Debebe Eshetu, Eskinder Nega, and Andualem Aragie is just the latest reminder that it is very dangerous to criticize the government in Ethiopia."

This is what the 2013 Human Rights Practices Report of the United

States Department of State reported about some of the above-mentioned journalists and newspaper publishers:

On January 17, authorities arrested Solomon Kebede, columnist and managing editor of *Muslim Affairs*. They charged him along 27 other Muslims in April under the antiterrorism proclamation. The case against Tesesgen Dessalegn, editor of the defunct *Feteh* newspapaer, continued. Charges against him included inciting and agitating the country's youth to engage in violence, defamation of the government, and destabilizing the public by spreading false reports. Mastewal Berhanu, former publisher and newspaper director of *Feteh*, reportedly left the country due to government harassment.

All told, by 2015 there are 21 journalists and bloggers charged; from these 21 journalists 18 are in prison and 3 charged an absentia. More than 30 journalists (twice the number of exiles documented by the CPJ in 2012 and 2013 combined) are in exile, thereby making Ethiopia one of the top ten journalist jailers in the world. According to *Reporters Without Borders* (2014), Ethiopia ranks 137th on the 2013 World Press Index; in 2014 Ethiopia ranked 143rd out of 180 countries.

Basically, prosecutors use documents of government criticism as evidence against journalists, bloggers, and dissenting politicians. Several Opposition political leaders (mainly young politicians), are also imprisoned accused of or charged with terrorism and other grave crimes.
Almost all journalists, bloggers, and politicians mentioned above are victims of the Anti-Terrorism Law of the country. The charges are indicative of the Ethiopian government's way of misusing this law to smother free speech and the functioning of free media.

Political, administrative and legal measures have been taken to weaken the economic capacity of private press publishers. The measures include a five-fold increase in the price of imported paper and ink which has resulted in the bankruptcy of many publishers.

Berhannena Selam Printing Enterprise, the country's largest printing establishment, applies a "Publication Standard Contract Agreement". Article 10(1) of this contract states that "the printing press may, when it has a reason to believe that there is illegal content on the material, refuse service to the publisher.", demonstrating that *Berhannena Selam* censors material before it gets to be printed. This is a measure taken by the ruling party to bar material from being printed and circulated. A side-effect is that more and more private presses have to fold. This is yet another method to strengthen the authoritarian regime.

Article 10(2) of the Publication Standard Contract Agreement states that "the printing press may, when it has a reason to believe that the material's content is potentially capable to entail liability, refuse service to the publisher." This implies not only the official authorization of censorship, but also the unlawfulness of the free press. It also clearly violates the provision of 9(1) of the Constitution. Needless to say, The *Berhannena Selam Printing Enterprise* is directly under the supervision of the ruling party and it is led by officials of the government.

_ 1.4 Self-Censorship

The private media is being forced to follow the patterns of the public media through *self-censorship* which is caused by fear of prosecution. In addition, the private media is barred from credit services from government and private banks. In short, the private media is operating under a severe challenge. The media policy applied by the ruling party intends to frustrate the operation of the private media, and – thus – to silence alternative views. Arresting private media owners and journalists who dare to challenge the system and the prosecution that follows, act as a deterrent; hence the application of self-censorship. In the modern information era self-censorship should be banned as it affects the freedom of expression and it hinders technological innovation and creativity at large. This is so because freedom of speech and expression constitute the pillars of human being's identity and of progress and development.

Terje Skjerdal wrote an article about self-censorship in Ethiopia. In essence his article documents self-censorship practices in three state-owned media institutions: (i) Ethiopian Television, (ii) the Ethiopian News Agency, and, (iii) the Ethiopian Herald. [1]

---

1 Terje Skjerdal (2011): **Development Journalism Revived: the Case of Ethiopia**; 74(2011). http://www.tandfonline.com/doi/abs

The data from in-depth interviews with 34 reporters and editors reveals that self-censorship is an everyday activity in the newsrooms. Moreover, it is particularly prevalent during times of tension and in the coverage of political stories.

The article discusses how self-censorship is internalized and reinforced among new candidates for reporter jobs. It is argued that the journalists take on certain "ethical rationalizations" (or pseudo ethical reasoning) to justify self-censorship.

_ 1.5 Ethical and Political Roles of the Government in Media

Media establishment in any country depends on relevant laws of the country concerned and on realities on the ground. This means that media should follow an editorial policy that doesn't contradict the Constitution and laws pertaining to the media. The editorial policy should be fine-tuned based on: a) the principles of the profession, and, b) the country's legal framework.

The media operates on the basis of its editorial policy; journalists are expected to be aware of the policy and regulations concerned. This means that the editorial policy should be crafted in a way that upholds the principles of journalism.

The relative progress of the free press during the period 1993-2005 didn't continue. In contemporary Ethiopia, the major hindrances for a free press are creations of the government.

Clearly, the government is not paying attention to enhance the establishment of alternative media, such as independent radio and TV stations. Rather, it is focusing on ensuring a monopoly of information sources. This attitude not only reduces the likelihood of finding alternative sources of information in a society, but it also creates a monotonous society, in that the public is not allowed to take in information from independent sources of information and to give feedback.

The time and budget spent by the EPRDF regime to undermine free media could have been used to build useful public institutions in the country. Instead, the regime doesn't create a positive enabling environment for independent media. The ruling party's program clearly shows that all media print or broadcast are expected to serve the cause and ideology of EPRDF —

revolutionary democracy and the developmental state paradigm.

Thus, in light of the political ideology of the system, it is evident from the regime's attitude towards free media that it has no interest to build an open and democratic society. However, democracy cannot be realized without the free press.

The above strategies were not planned in 2005, yet they are a continuation of the party's original politico-economic policy since assuming state power in 1991. During the transitional period from 1991 to 1994, the regime adopted Press Proclamation 34/93 to recognize freedom of the press only to portray itself to Western donors that it was committed to democracy and press freedom so that donors would continue their support to the new regime.

Although at first freedom of the press was in good shape, as it was supported not only by the proclamation but also by the Constitution, EPRDF started to close many presses after losing the 2005 election. True, it is undeniable that there was insufficient journalistic professionalism and ethics on the part of the infant private press. But the main culprit in the downward spiral of freedom of the press is the regime, for it has put into effect draconic administrative, legal, and political instruments to undermine, if not to eliminate, the free press.

The major obstacles for the implementation of the free press in Ethiopia are the lack of due understanding of the importance and meaning of the free press by the ruling party, and the creation of direct and indirect obstacles for its functioning. The opposition parties are also to be blamed as they also criticize the free media for exposing their shortcomings and misdeeds.

Balance, impartiality, truthfulness, and credibility are at the foundation of the profession of journalism. Institutions that provide training and capacity building should be recommending that journalists stick to the principles of the profession, instead of being loyal to groups and political parties that contrast with the basic principles and ethics of journalism.

_ 1.6 Mass Media and Democracy

Mass media and democracy complement each other. A society that freely expresses its views and that has built up the tradition of transparency can realize a country that is known for its strong democracy and good governance.

In any given society, the absence of checks and balances provided by free and independent media can easily lead to dictatorial rule. Without the existence of a well-informed society it is impossible to respect the *Rule of Law*, nor to attain social transformation and inclusive development. Instead, everything will be judged based on the interests of the ruling party, which – in turn –creates a parasitic society where people live by the principles of opportunism. That is why corruption, embezzlement of public money, and illegal business practices constitute the day-to-day reality in Ethiopia.

_ 1.7 The Role of Social Media

Social media makes the flow of information smooth, efficient, as well as instant. Facebook, Twitter, LinkedIn, and Google are contributing a lot to social interaction, thereby greatly enhancing the freedom of expression. However, social media has also drawbacks, such as information that raises questions about credibility, and dissemination of information that is morally unacceptable.

Social media can only flourish – and benefit society – if it is free from censorship. Internet freedom, however, is a relative phenomenon in Ethiopia. This is what the US State Department's 2013 Human Rights Perception Report observed: 'The government blocked access to the internet and blocked several websites, including blogs; opposition websites... Websites such as Facebook, Twitter, and Yahoo! were temporarily inaccessible at times. More than 65 news blogs and websites run by opposition diaspora groups, some international media, local journalists, bloggers, and activists who criticized and exposed the country's poor governance and human rights record were not accessible. These included *Addis Neger, Ethiopian Review, Ethiomedia, Nazareth, Zehabesha, Aljazeera, Cyber Ethiopia, Quatero Amharic Magazine, Tensae Ethiopia,* and the *Ethiopian Media Forum.*'

The good news is that citizen journalism makes use of the possibilities created by technological advances in electronic information transfer. Section 3.3 (pages 31/2) describes what citizen journalism entails.

/ CHAPTER TWO

ETHIOPIA'S ECONOMIC DEVELOPMENT SINCE THE 1990S

This chapter is about the importance of free media in pursuit of economic development. The term economic development has a wider connotation than economic growth. The difference between the two will be briefly explained. Large scale land sales and land leases (i.e., land grabbing) are being undertaken by the Ethiopian government. The importance of *checks and balances* – and the lack of them – in analyzing and documenting these land sales and leases is described in this chapter as well. The chapter ends with a presentation of the atrocities that took place in the Gambella Region.

_ 2.1. Economic Growth and Economic Development

This is what economic textbooks tell us about the two terms. Economic growth can be measured by an increase in a country's Gross Domestic Product (GDP). The term economic growth is a *narrower* concept than economic development It is an increase in a country's real level of national output resulting from an increase in the quantity and quality of resources, such as education and improvements in technology, or an increase in the value of goods and services produced by the country concerned. Economic growth doesn't take into account the depletion of natural resources which might lead to pollution, congestion & disease.

Economic development includes an increase in living standards, improvement in self-esteem, needs and freedom from oppression as well as a greater choice. Economic development also leads to the creation of more opportunities in the sectors of education, healthcare, employment and the conservation of the environment. It implies an increase in the per capita income of every citizen. Development alleviates people from low standards of living into proper employment and decent housing. Development is also concerned with sustainability, which means meeting the needs of the present without compromising future needs.

Economic growth is a necessary but not sufficient condition of economic development; so there can be growth but no development, in the sense as described above. Ethiopia registers robust growth figures. For example, the World Bank reported that the country grew 8.5% in 2013, which by all standards is an impressive achievement. However, more than 76 million Ethiopians still are poor; Ethiopia is the second poorest country in the world. Another indication that growth and development don't necessarily function in tandem, is Ethiopia's position on the Human Development Index (HDI) list, which measures the level of development rather than only economic growth.[2] The 2014 list included 187 countries. Ethiopia is number 173 on the list; hence a very low score. Norway occupies first place, by the way.

In the development literature, development is thus considered as a sum total of positive changes in human life. It includes political, social and economic changes and environmental protection. Development creates the opportunity to fulfill basic needs, and citizens can enjoy happy and healthy life. Positive socio-political and economic change promotes prosperity and well-being.

However, for the realization of this change to happen, commitment of the political leaders and the application of participatory development policies are of paramount importance. Economic growth and human development should act hand-in-hand in order to realize meaningful development. The developed countries have demonstrated how this can be done. In Ethiopia, the political leadership's focus is on economic growth, and not also on economic development.

Countries that assured economic development have fulfilled the basic needs of their people, provided good housing, and adequate health, education, and social protection services. Countries that are developing should follow a path from growth to development. If there is a political commitment to consistently follow that path, development – in the sense as mentioned above – can be achieved.

---

2 HDI criteria are: life expectancy at birth, mean years of schooling, expected years of schooling, and gross national income per capita.

Many researchers point out that natural resources are the basic inputs for economic development. Others believe that capable human beings are of great significance; they argue that, regardless of the existence or non-existence of natural resources, human beings are the principal source of economic development. They claim that countries having huge natural resources like some African countries are still backward in economic development, as they suffer from the *natural resource curse*.

_ 2.2 Economic Development in Ethiopia

Ethiopia, as noted, registers robust growth. Even though its HDI scores are low, there have also been positive changes in the country. During the regime of Menilik II there has been investment in infrastructure and in technology. Studies show that 67% of the country's economic growth is dominated by the government. Where there is a weak private sector and civil society, the participation of citizens in politics and in the economy is low. This creates dependency on the government and blurs the vision on the requirements of genuine economic development.

To promote economic development a government needs to know *how* to bring about economic development and how to mobilize the necessary resources. The Ethiopian government doesn't seem to have that knowledge. Where there isn't that knowledge, the government's efforts can never have a long-term development impact.

_ 2.3 Nature and Goal of the Developmental State

The ideology of a developmental state is to transform an agricultural economy into an industrial one, led by a government with a long-term vision. The classic economic philosophy of the developmental state marginalized human rights, including the freedom of speech and press.

The ideology was first introduced by Chalmers Johnson. The concept was to create a strong, meritocratic, government which would direct the development process at the detriment of private sector initiative, thereby weakening the functioning of the free market. This ideology would eventually lead to autocratic government.

Economic independence is the goal of the developmental state. This would be achieved by the promotion and protection of newly emerging local industries, with the help of imported technology. Government would provide the necessary infrastructure.

A different economic philosophy was applied by e.g. Japan, Singapore, Hong Kong, South Korea, Taiwan, and – later – China, resulted in phenomenal successes. Ethiopia and other African countries are now implementing elements of this ideology as well, taking into consideration the various cultural contexts in which South Africa, Brazil, India, Botswana, and the like, practice their own economic philosophy. These countries strongly focus on their private sectors, emphasize human and democratic rights, and the free market.

_ 2.4 Is Ethiopia a Developmental State?

The powers that be claim that Ethiopia has gradually become a developmental state.

According to the developmental state philosophy, public services should be delivered efficiently. Public service providers, including their managers, should be capable professionals, and be selected - not because of their loyalty to the ruling party – but on the basis of meritocratic principles. This is unfortunately not the case in Ethiopia. Leading ministers, vice ministers, directors, managers, down to districts, are in some cases illiterate. Accountability mechanisms regarding public service delivery are in fact non-existent. As regards education, in its 23 years of governing, the EPRDF regime has hardly educated people with any practical skill. University graduates have difficulties to find a job, not only because the jobs are in short supply but especially also because they lack the minimum qualifications for the vacancies on hand.

Economic activities in the country are performed with direct order and control from the government, and they are not based on hearings or participation of citizens.

For the EPRDF's state model to be called a developmental state, it has to focus much more on political and institutional change, rather than focusing merely on economic growth. EPRDF has demonstrated over the past 24 years that the government has no capacity to bring about positive changes in political, economic, and social conditions of the country. The same applies to environmental issues. As for the distribution of incomes and wealth, there is a big economic gap between the rich (those affiliated with the party and the party's businesses) and the poor who have remained voiceless.

For development to be achieved, the issue of political, social, and economic transformation has to be emphasized. For this to happen all citizens have to have a say, while government leads the way. If not, development will remain a fantasy.

_ 2.5 Land Policies, Human Rights, Land Grabbing, and the Role of the Media

2.5.1 Land Policies

Ethiopia belongs to the league of countries that has not ensured food security. The country's land policy is based upon the right of landownership by the government (which took it from the society). This affects the productivity of local and indigenous farmers. The current government has allocated vast amounts of land to foreigners for a period of 30 to 50 years. According to Desalegn Rahmato (2011), large tracts of fertile lands were transferred to foreigners in Ethiopia from 2003 to 2009. Most of the lands were given to investors displacing the land owners of indigenous society, without adequate public consultation nor any form of compensation. So far, these land allocations apparently focused on earning foreign currency rather than assuring the country's food security.

2.5.2 Human Rights

Development and human rights are interrelated. Where there is development, there is respect for human rights. This is not the case in Ethiopia. Particularly since 2005, human rights are being violated, including those in connection with land transfers. Nonetheless, the Constitution under Article 40(3) claims that the right to ownership of rural and urban land, as well as of all natural resources, is exclusively vested in the nations, nationalities, and peoples of Ethiopia so that it shall not be subject to sale or to other means of exchange. [3] The same Article 40, sub-articles 4 and 5, states that Ethiopian peasants have the right to obtain land without payment and protection against eviction from their possessions while specifying that the implementation of the provision are to be specified by law.

Some studies suggest that large-scale land transfers were inspired by the tragic famines of 1973 and 1984 during which many people died. [4] The government became more open to the introduction of a commercial-scale green revolution, supported by development agencies such as the World Bank, the British Department for International Development (DFID), and the African Development Bank.

Investment zones were opened to foreign private investors. One example concerned highland floriculture investments by Dutch companies. This was done without dispossessions, as there was sufficient land available. Ethiopia's Poverty Reduction Strategy Paper (PRSP) gave another boost to fresh investments in land; this time in lowland areas, traditionally inhabited by pastoralists applying shifting cultivation.

2.5.3 Land Grabbing

From 2009-2010, large tracts of fertile lands were leased to foreigners. A vast amount of forest was destroyed. In the process, violation of human rights against the indigenous communities occurred.

Ethiopian pastoralists – as noted – have the right to free land for grazing and cultivation as well as the protection of displacement from their own lands. However, many who had lived in the vicinity of cities were displaced by government without proper compensation. The government's rationale for moving pastoralists from their ancestral lands was that their farming was not sustainable; their livelihoods should be improved

3 However, Article 3(1) of Proclamation 455 (2005) states that the district administrator has the power to expropriate lands and evict peasants from them on the grounds that the lands in question are needed for public purposes, or will be more valuable if they are utilized by private investors, cooperative societies or 'other bodies'.
4 Makki, F. and Geisler, C.(2011) Paper presented at the Global Land Grabbing Conference. Sussex.

by creating job opportunities elsewhere, according to the Minister of Agriculture and Rural Development. His Ministry is the principal body for negotiations on land leases above 5,000 ha. Close to 4 million ha of land have been allocated and transferred to international investors by this Ministry (Annexe III includes an overview of land allocations)

These ancestral lands were transferred to foreign investors and members of the ruling party, either for free or for a cheap price, without prior permission from affected farmers and pastoralists. When they claimed their rights, the government often branded them as anti-development and anti-peace-loving. The government defended its actions arguing that the displacement was done with the consent of local communities, although the latter never had a chance to protest. Instead, they were often forced to speak on the state media in favour of the displacement. Independent media and other international investigators of human rights abuses were prohibited from visiting the sites of displacement.

2.5.4 The Gambella Case

A land grabbing/displacement case in point concerns the Gambella Region. In this region 225,000 indigenous communities have been forcefully displaced to date. According to a report of the Oakland Institute (2011), the clash between government forces and local communities there constituted a gross violation of human rights. 424 Anuak community members died, while others were imprisoned and tortured. Between 8,000 and 10,000 people reportedly fled the country.

It all started in 2009 when the government published a brochure to attract large-scale investors with the offer that 1.2 million ha of unused land was available in the Gambella region. The World Bank undertook research to identify areas with growth potential within the Gambella region. This potential was to be enhanced by public investments (i.e., roads, electricity, and water supply) so as to contribute to economic growth. Makki and Geisler noted, while admitting that: the current regime in Ethiopia is not pro-large-corporations: '... [i]t definitely is pro-development and committed to a classical notion of development that once informed the national projects of newly independent post-colonial states'[5]

In preparation of the influx of foreign investors, peasants and pastoralists were evicted or transferred to other places. One example concerns the semi-nomadic Nuer people: they were forcibly transferred to Bildak, a new village in the Gambella region. The Nuer quickly abandoned Bildak in May 2011 because there was no water source for their cattle. The Anuak refugees issued a complaint alleging that the Bank violated its own safeguards in Gambella. The case was taken up by the Bank's independent Inspection Panel which concluded that the Bank indeed violated its own policies in Ethiopia.

Jessica Evans, Human Rights Watch's senior international financial institutions researcher, concluded that the Inspection Panel's report showed that the World Bank had largely ignored human rights risks evident in its projects in Ethiopia. The Bank now has the opportunity and responsibility to adjust course on its Ethiopia programming and provide redress to those who were harmed. But management's Action Plan achieves neither, according to Evans.

2.5.5 The Role of the Media

The local media's role has been minimal because the Ethiopian government would not tolerate honest reporting on the Gambella and Southern lower Omo case. Thanks to the fact that organizations like Human Rights Watch (HRW) investigated the case, and that HRW was able to draw international attention, the World Bank's Inspection Panel reacted favorably. So, without the assistance of HRW and the international media attention, the human rights violations in the Gambella Region would not have been exposed and attended to.

As for the lower Omo case mentioned above, 200,000 indigenous farmers were displaced by force, without adequate public consultation, and compensation.

---

5 *Development by Dispossession*, p. 15.

/ CHAPTER THREE

CAN JOURNALISM PLAY ITS PROFESSIONAL ROLE IN ETHIOPIA'S DEVELOPMENT?

Journalism can be defined as a profession that utilizes mass media technologies in an effort to gather, research, categorize, evaluate, analyze, and disseminate relevant information on current issues. The person who discharges those responsibilities is referred to as journalist.

Information presented by journalist from a credible source will have an effect on society, positive or otherwise. This requires caution from the part of journalists. Because any wrong information not only undermines the profession, but it may even cause grave calamity, including unforeseen damage to the country and the population.

Journalism, as a profession, requires abstaining from party affiliation and avoiding any temptation based on selfish interests, since the profession demands that the journalist shall be loyal to the society he serves. This doesn't mean that a journalist cannot have personal views, including political views and/or religious beliefs. But the difference is that he/she should maintain a balance: and draw a line between his personal life on the one hand and professional duties on the other. If not, he/she will undermine the credibility of the media, and cannot earn the respect and trust of society.

So, the primary role of journalists working in mass media should be providing credible information in a way that is balanced in an effort to inform, educate, enlighten, and motivate their society. The legal protection given to the profession and journalists depends on the laws of the country concerned and on the political ideologies of the party - or parties - that rule the nation.

_ 3.1. From Amateur to Professional Journalism
For many years passionate individuals, without much formal education

were able to play the role of journalists. Previous regimes took advantage of the knowledge gap; hence the 'amateur' journalists did not have any other option than to follow strict orders from the people who were in power. It was unlikely that such journalists would have the courage and capacity to challenge the status-quo at the time.

Journalism is now recognized as a true profession. Journalism is being taught at higher education institutions in the country. Currently, graduate and post-graduate courses are being given at various universities, such as Addis Ababa University, Bahir Dar University, Hawassa University, and Mekelle University, among others. [6] Unfortunately, many years have passed without any signs of improvement of professional standards. One reason is that professional journalists are moving to other fields for their own safety and/or to earn a better income.

_ 3.2 Development Journalism in Ethiopia

Development journalism was first introduced in 1960s in The Philippines. The journalists who introduced it were Alan Chalkley and Juan Mercado. It gained popularity among developing country regimes. Development journalism represents the kind of journalism in which the journalist reports on development activities, as well as on issues relating to the quality and coverage of education, health, agriculture, and the like.

The objective of development journalism is to foster inclusive and equitable socio-economic development through public participation. This type of journalism also intends to propose remedies to challenges, and to provide executive bodies with popular feedback so that bottlenecks are removed.

The approach taken is a *bottom-up approach*, since the issues are gathered by researching the activities on the ground. When properly implemented, development journalism can contribute significantly to social and economic transformation processes in developing countries. It also helps in creating awareness of government policies among communities, and this helps in enhancing participation and fostering a sense of ownership among them.

6 The basic principles of journalism are included in Annexe IV.

Another objective is to conduct research, to follow up ongoing development activities, as well as to provide status updates to the population. This helps in realizing accountability and responsiveness of the authorities, as the recommendations forwarded by society and stakeholders are assumed to be implemented by those responsible for the activities researched.

Development journalism shares similar principles as those of the free press, and it has the objective of ensuring social justice, equity and mutual prosperity in an effort to serve the best interest of society. This doesn't mean that the model of development journalism differs from the free press, collaborative, or citizen journalism, or any other journalistic model. Rather development journalism resembles the model of the free press and private media, since all of them work towards the goal of ensuring social justice and equity, based upon public participation. Universally accepted values and principles of journalism are fully applicable to development journalism.

Now, what is the reality of development journalism in Ethiopia? As regards the application of development journalism one can say that it has been implemented without any awareness of its basic bottom-up approach. In Ethiopia the ruling party has taken advantage of the prevailing knowledge gap among various stakeholders. It has been continuously manipulating the state-owned media, including the Ethiopia Radio and Television Agency, the Ethiopia News Agency, the Ethiopian Press Agency, as well as the regional radio stations. The party is utilizing them as propaganda tools to promote their Revolutionary Democracy ideology. Hence, the ruling party is manipulating the prevailing knowledge gap to undermine the principles of development journalism in an effort to meet its own interests and those of the elites.

Terje Skejrdal conducted research on the issue of development journalism in Ethiopia. [7] He analyzed what happened to the Ethiopian government's intention to establish development journalism as the official reporting style since 2008. This intention was inspired by the fact that, as noted above, development journalism became popular among

Skjerdal, T.S. (2011) Development Journalism Revived: The Case of Ethiopia; 74 (2011); http://www.tandfonline.com/doi/abs

African governments as a way to utilize the media for social and national growth. Skjerdal interviewed several journalists in-depth, and he compared Ethiopia's practice with other development journalism models. He came to the conclusion that although the journalists are favorable towards development journalism as a professional framework, they have difficulties converting this framework into actual media practice. Skjerdal identified three problems regarding this conversion: (i) the ambiguity of development journalism as a concept and practice: (ii) the political inclination of the state media, and, (iii) a lack of participation by the public.

Skjerdal mentioned about the ambiguity the following:

Implementation of development journalism turns out to be marked by top-down directives rather than participation from below. This is in great contrast to old and new theories of development journalism. In the Ethiopian case, both the policy document and the journalists speak warmly of the importance of people-driven journalism; but ultimately it is leaders and managers who frame the nature and extent of such participation.

The ruling party has been continuously making efforts to silence alternative voices when it comes to entertaining diverse political views in the state media. As a result, the state media have been violating the basic principles of the profession. The top leaders of the ruling party have been acting in manner that violates professional principles by drawing an ambiguous line between journalism and public relations while distorting facts in their favour to safeguard political gains.

Regarding the role of public relations, public relation experts, particularly in government organizations, are supposed to create a bridge for information between government institutions and the general public. Even though their primary role is communicating information, heads of public relations in Ethiopian governmental institutions are not willing to give information which may be damaging to the government's image. As a result, they don't provide information about, for example, the imprisonment of journalists. So, government public relations bureaus create a formidable obstacle to journalists' access to information.

If there was a political atmosphere that encourages the implementation of development journalism, problems would have been resolved before it was too late, and citizens would have been proud of being Ethiopians. The Ethiopian people are kind and generous when it comes to joining hands and supporting each other in times of crises and calamity. However, the lack of transparency and the application of double standards by the government are making the lives of citizens more difficult.

The leaders of the ruling party seem to be intentionally ignorant and out of touch when it comes to identifying and responding to the needs of the citizens. They have been misleading them through the state media. Utilizing the state media for the purpose of propaganda will lead to wasting scarce resources, including air time and human capital, which is paid for by tax revenues from ordinary Ethiopians.

_ 3.3 Citizen Journalism

Mark Glazer takes the credit for the introducing the theory of citizen journalism. He reckons that, this type of journalism enables the general public to access information from different sources, in addition to mainstream media. The contemporary era is known for the ever increasing eagerness for information; everyone wants to read and watch new tips, features, personal stories, including on Facebook, Twitter, Google+, blogs, and LinkedIn. The international flow of information is favouring information from alternative sources. As every community has its own distinct nature, citizen journalism can provide a custom-made model of journalism which may be useful to ensure a sense of ownership among the local communities.

Modern technologies, including smart phones, have contributed to the fast acceptance of citizen journalism as a new model for the ever increasing attention it is getting from various stakeholders, including progressive politicians. These politicians are utilizing the new media to communicate with their supporters. And at the same time they gather useful feedback from them.

The people around the world have been able to exchange opinions, views, and to learn from best practices of other communities. The use of blogs as platforms to reach out to a heterogeneous target audiences online promotes the habit of reading. Citizen journalism can greatly contribute to the awareness of major political, economic, human rights, or environmental issues.

Terry Flew, who is a specialist on the new media, suggests three reasons for the fast growth and acceptance of citizen journalism: (i) free and transparent transmission, (ii) collaborative alliances, and, (iii) the accessibility of content. Other analysts state that citizen journalism managed to penetrate into countries without a free press due to the fact that in the past the general public was unable to find information from different sources, since most of the authoritarian governments have been doing their level best to silence alternative voices.

In 1980, citizen journalism was introduced in Northern America, when forecasting the result of the American presidential election. The significance of citizen journalism was especially seen in Tunisia where the Arab revolution started, after Mohammed Buaziz burnt his body in protest against the Ben Ali regime. The role of this journalism reaches up to overthrowing dictatorial leaders. Sending photos of Mohammed Bouaziz's burnt body by mobile phones strengthened the peoples' revolt against the system, which made this form of citizen journalism successful in no time.

The beginning of the Arab revolution in Tunisia intensified the revolt in Egypt, Libya, Yemen, Algeria, Morocco, Bahrain and Saudi Arabia, which resulted in the downfall of the authoritarian regimes in Egypt, Libya, and Yemen.

The application of citizen journalism in Ethiopia is poor, with minimal participation. The main reasons for this are government's total control over the telecommunication services, government's hacking of various websites, inaccessibility of alternative telecom services, the unaffordability of government telecom services, the poor nature of the services' quality and accessibility. As a result, the population's interest in and usage of the technology is poor.

However if everybody can freely use the technology at hand, citizen journalism has great potential in information sharing and awareness-raising.

_ 3.4. The Role of Journalism in Ethiopia's democracy and development

In Ethiopia journalism has a big challenge to contribute to the development of the country and to help promote democratic governance. There are a number of limitations created by government bodies, the media atmosphere, and the country's political system, lack of professionalism, limited public awareness, and limited resources. The EPRDF regime is controlling all media technology and – on top of it – doesn't tolerate critics of the regime.

As noted above, journalists in Ethiopia work under self-censorship. Should a journalist wish to work free from government control, he/she has three options: (i) prison, (ii) exile, or, (iii) after all, accept government control. The sad conclusion is that – at the moment – there is no role for journalism to strengthen democracy and support Ethiopia's economic development because every independence-minded journalist or blogger will be closely monitored by the government. And as soon as he/she reports in a critical manner about government's actions, he/she will be silenced.

_ 3.5 The Role of Journalists Associations

The establishment of strong and neutral associations of journalists is vital for the protection of their freedom, safety, and rights, as well as for the improvement of their skills.

Journalists' associations also engage in capacity building by organizing various professional trainings. These associations are strong representatives of journalists' interests, and thus act as a meaningful bargaining power vis-a-vis the government, media institutions, and other stakeholders. These are the primary objectives of the associations.

In Ethiopia there are four accredited journalists associations: the Ethiopian National Journalists Union, the Science Journalists Association, the Ethiopian Journalists Association, and the Ethiopian Sport Journalists Association. Most of them are pro government and – therefore – are poor defenders of press freedom. Some of their leaders condemn journalists who try to report according to their own professional standards, and not on the basis of what their employers want to hear.

There was a valiant association before, i.e., the Ethiopian Free Journalists Association, which was led by Kifle Mulat. This association was dissolved after the leaders had been suppressed by the government; in 2013 its license was cancelled.

In short, what is left of the free press is suffering from intimidation, threats, and prosecution. Quite a few members of the free press were forced to live in exile.

The government has done its best to cheat the international community by pretending that citizens have the right of association. However, civil and professional associations have been the targets of the ruling party, it denies them proper registration and license.

In the past there were two associations who were denied a license – the Ethiopian Environmental Journalists and the Ethiopian Female Journalists Association – that made significant contributions to the defense of the free press. Among the associations that have been granted license and that are working for the interests of society and their members, the Ethiopian Sports Journalists Association should be mentioned.

However, much is yet to be done when it comes to ensuring the rights and liberty of the members of the journalism association. The majority of the still functioning associations are simply taking advantage of the journalists they claim to serve, as their leadership applies opportunistic tactics.

In an effort to fill this gap, on 30 January 2014 the Ethiopian Journalists Forum (EJF) was founded by 30 permanent members. A government representative, the British and American Embassies, and a representative of a local activist group, *Zone 9 Bloggers*, attended as observer the founding meeting.

However, as a result of government pressure, this association has not been able to get proper accreditation and license. The leaders of the above-listed associations also conspired against the members of the Forum. The result was that the government's Ethiopian Charity and Societies

Agency decided to refuse EJF a license. This story once again shows that the government doesn't want an independent associations of journalists.

Some of the founding members of the Forum have been easy targets of the state media who claimed that these founding members were terrorist supporters. The co-founder and members of EJF's executive board, Betre Yacob, Zerihun Mulugeta, Habtamu Seyoum, and Bisrat Woldemichael, went into exile in 2014.

The Committee for the Protection of Journalists, Reporters Without Borders, Article 19, and Freedom House, as well as PEN International Ethiopia have been campaigning for press freedom and for the freedom of expression in Ethiopia. Amnesty International and Human Rights Watch have been supporting the sacred cause of defending the rights of journalists and benefits of the free press.

These organizations, and others, have been publishing reports stating the level of problems of press freedom; some of them have rated the situation in Ethiopia as the worst. The reality on the ground is even worse than what has been reported by foreigners. What is ironic is that the central issues of press freedom and freedom of expression have not been addressed by the local associations of journalists, nor has any of them one them published a report stating the problem.

Since there is no Ethiopian association that truly stands for the rights of journalists, there are several drawbacks, including the issues of quality and lack of competence on the part of journalists. As a result, the majority of journalists working at print, electronic and online media are not really professional journalists; they are amateurs learning the skills and gaining knowledge along the way. This undermines the profession, and it may fuel the current trend where journalists have extreme views and pull issues to the opposite poles, rather than coming together and creating mutual understanding.

In such circumstances the general public suffers a lot, since it will be impossible to have access to credible, balanced, and relevant information on issues that affect the lives of people and – in the end – Ethiopia's future development.

The ruling party is responsible for the above-stated problems. The associations that claim to stand for the rights of journalists also contributed to the political and other hindrances that undermine the profession. The principles of the profession have been sidelined due to unethical practices of opportunists. Realizing free and independent media, that doesn't surrender to be parasitic s and that is not fooled by false promises, is the only road to positive change. Journalism should be a profession where competition and competence is the key to success. Journalists should be eager to adapt to new technologies and to move forward to reach the heights of their cherished profession and thus better contribute to Ethiopia's development.

/ CHAPTER FOUR
CONCLUSION AND RECOMMENDATIONS

Even though Ethiopia has a long history and a long governmental system, the country hasn't got a government that is elected by the free will of the people. The government should rule its citizens impartially and equally. However, the government has divided the people into two contradictory groups and this has become a hindrance for the unity, peace, and development of the country. The ones who oppose the system are labeled as anti-peace, anti-development, anti-democracy elements, or terrorists.

The prevailing government's structure is devoid of transparency, responsibility, and accountability. It is based on ethnicity. The government should, according to the Constitution, allow freedom of the press, organization, and the freedom to express one's views.

Institutions such as the Courts, Police and Security, Media, the Electoral Board, and civic institutions must be neutral, impartial, and independent. However, the government fully controls the mass media and does not allow optional ideas or free opinion. In this environment, journalists have only four options: (i) to apply self-censorship, (ii) go into exile, (iii) get imprisoned, or, (iv) copy the government's ideas and interests.

In Ethiopia it is impossible to express one's views freely; there is no freedom of the press, the right to organize, or to gather in freedom.

19 Journalists and bloggers, several political party leaders (including party members) and religious leaders have been jailed so far. Even some regional members of political parties have been arrested; nobody knows their whereabouts.

There are many blocked voices that may erupt any time like a volcanic eruption, which may plunge the country into a very unstable situation. Therefore, the institutional shortcomings mentioned above should be addressed by the government. Freedom of the press and freedom of expression, as enshrined in the Constitution, should be ensured; indeed, free from the domination and control of the ruling party.

The government must respect the supremacy of the law and act accordingly. The government must respect the Constitution. Press freedom and freedom of speech are inseparable and must be implemented, rather than remaining a dead letter.

Everyone has to be concerned about the impact of censorship in all aspects of human activity and development.

The government should revise the Anti-Terrorism Law.

Ethiopia's donors should express more concern about human rights violation and give the issue more priority in their assistance policies. This may help in preventing the imminent political and social crisis from erupting, including its possible spreading to Horn of African states.

The Environmental and Social Impact Assessment Law should be applied to investment programs, in particular to land investment programs.

Regarding large land investment programs, donors and foreign investors should demonstrate genuine concern for the human rights of affected populations, and for environmental aspects.

Journalists, politicians, and religious leaders must be free to express their opinion. Censorship and discrimination must be stopped.

By giving priority to human development, rather than material development, the government will then also promote the protection of basic human rights.

Besides, the government must carefully review its policies and amend some of them, with a view to promote the development of all Ethiopians.

Finally, everybody must carefully take note of these conclusions and recommendations and propose and/or implement solutions and remedies before things get out of, so that Ethiopia will transform into a free, open, and prosperous nation.

ANNEXE I

The Nature and Evolution of the Ethiopian State and Government

The Ethiopian state originates from the 1st AD, i.e., during the Axumite Kingdom in Northern Ethiopia, which was then called Abyssinia. Axum was also one of the oldest civilizations thereby making Ethiopia one of the oldest states in the world. The Axumite dynasty was weakened by the expansion of Arabs and Islam.

The decline of Axum gave way to Queen Yodit (Judith) who was a follower of the conservative Jewish religion. Queen Judith ruled the country for 40 years. Judith's power was usurped by the Zagwe (Agaw) dynasty which moved their capital from Axum to Lasta Lalibela in central Wollo province. The Zagwe dynasty stayed in power from 900-1270 A.D. After the decline of the Zagwe, the Solomonic dynasty followed when King Yukuno Amilak restored the Solomonic and Yeju dynasty based in Gonder, in the central province of Shewa. Finally, Solomonic dynasty stayed in power from 1271-1974 A.D until Emperor Hailesselassie I was deposed.

Attempts of centralization of the Ethiopian state against several semi-autonomous feudal provinces began during Emperor Tewodros II (1855-1868) who ended long years of the Era of Princes (locally known as the *Zamana Mesafint*). It was in the late 20th century that Ethiopia became a centralized state during Emperor Menelik II, who ruled the country from the late 1880s until 1913. Emperor Haileselassie I, who ruled the country from 1930 to 1974, also pursued a strong policy of centralization and consolidation of state power.

Ethiopia adopted its first ever Constitution in 1931. The Emperor introduced a bicameral parliament – namely the Senate and Chamber of Deputies – designated under his absolute monarchy.

However, due to the unresolved questions of land, ethnicity, and democracy, the student movement against the monarchy gained momentum in the 1960s. A spontaneous social revolution broke out in 1974 and toppled the Emperor. However, the student movement and clandestine political parties were not well organized at the time. Thus, following the overthrow of the monarchy, a military junta called hijacked the revolution and assumed state power by using the power vacuum.

The Dergue soon proclaimed their Marxism Leninism inclinations, and introduced radical socio-economic and political changes, thereby making Ethiopia a socialist state. The Dergue had promised to transform the country into a democratic state. Yet it was only in 1987 that the Dergue adopted a Constitution which made Ethiopia a Peoples' Democratic Republic. In the first general popular election ever, Colonel Mengisutu Hailemariam, chairman of the Dergue, was the only presidential candidate, and so he was elected President of the Republic.

The Dergue was challenged in civil war by ethnic liberation fronts in Eritrea, Ogaden and Tigray. Finally, Tigray people's liberation front, TPLF formed a coalition with other ethnic groups, such as the Amhara National Democratic Movement (ANDM) and Oromo Peoples' Democratic Organization (OPDO).

They established the Ethiopian Peoples' Revolutionary Democratic Front (EPRDF), which toppled the military regime in May 1991. After controlling Addis Ababa, EPRDF incorporated another member party from the South namely the South Ethiopian Peoples' Democratic Front (SEPDF), which later became the South Ethiopian Peoples' Democratic Movement (SPDM). EPRDF has also affiliate ethnic parties in the Somali, Afar, Harari, Gambella and Benshangul-Gumuz regions; they are all members of EPRDF. Their activities are controlled and led by the EPRDF.

Since 1991, Ethiopia is a multiethnic federal state whereas the form of government is a multi-party parliamentary democracy.

Following the coming into effect of the Constitution of the Federal Democratic Republic of Ethiopia in 1995, it made Ethiopia a multi-ethnic federal state with a parliamentary form of government. EPRDF redrew the Ethiopian state along ethnic federalism lines.

So far, four general elections were conducted in which various political parties took part. However, the elections have never been free and fair by all international standards.

The autonomous nine regional states are all under the EPRDF control, either through member or affiliated parties. Therefore, all regions have lost their constitutional autonomy as overall directions come from the central government and the ruling party at the center; it is typically a top-down approach of democratic centralism. As a result, the regional governments are not accountable to their people but to the EPRDF at the center. In other words, the system has curtailed the implementation of genuine multi-party federalism. Instead, what has prevailed in Ethiopia is basically an authoritarian and centralized system under the coercive hegemony of one ethnic-based leftist party.

The Constitution also established three organs of government, i.e., the Executive (the Prime Minister and the Council of Ministers), the Legislative, and the Judiciary.

The legislative organ is composed of a bicameral parliament, namely the House of Peoples Representatives and the House of Federation. With its various standing committees the house is expected to discharge and ratify laws and proclamations that serve the interest of society without any prejudice in an effort to ensure social justice, equity and inclusive development.

The representatives may be elected form one party or from various parties in a free and fair open ballot box conducted every five years. The party that wins the majority seats forms a government. Minority parties are allowed to have the right of forwarding policy alternatives and suggest remedies, so that the interest for the various groups is considered.

Members of the House are accountable to the general population they represent, to the Constitution, and to their conscience. However, when the members of the House of Peoples' Representatives act in a manner that undermines their legitimacy, it damages the interest of the people. When their actions violate the Constitution, the population has the right to remove them through a system of recall. In reality, however, representatives of the House are often accountable to their parties in a way that contradicts with the Constitution.

The power of interpreting the Constitution is given to the House of Federation, whose members are elected by the executive members from all regional councils. In terms of procedure, they can be selected directly or indirectly from each recognized ethnic group in the country, i.e., all ethnic groups have at least one representative. This raises the question of the interpretation of the constitution by a political body instead of the country's Supreme Court or an independent Constitutional Court. Therefore, the accountability of members of the House of Federation is not to their conscience and ethnic groups they claim to represent, but only to the ruling party which has brought them to the legislative organ in the first place Thus, it is habitual to see the Constitution being violated and interpreted in accordance with the wishes of the executive body.

The federal government structure in Ethiopia is not accountable to the people but to the party which rules the country. And therefore, it is quite opposite to the objective of the federal system formation. This is because the administrators who are in the federal structure do not have their own independence. Their leaders are not elected by the people but by the will and permission of the highest and supreme power in the federal government.

A federal administration which is based on geographical location and settlement of people is preferable to bring equity in power, culture, and language among the communities involved. It is also preferable because it allows equal distribution of resources. In particular, it helps to preserve national integrity and security, freedom, and equality. It minimizes internal conflicts between borders, corruption, and narrow nationalism. The negative side is that does give a chance to some backward, racist, and selfish people, who suffer from a superiority complex and belittle other people.

The federal system, which is based on language and culture, is a system which serves new countries which do not have a common ancient history and cultural ties among themselves and enables them to get along with each other. This system has a negative impact for Ethiopians who have an ancient history, culture, and social interaction. This is because it enables the citizens not to have equality and reliability among themselves, one to dominate the other and be hostile, create border conflicts, and risk the unity and security of the country. In particular, if a federal government is formed based on languages, the minority ethnic groups may be discriminated, victimized, and alienated by the majority ethnic group. This is extensively seen in Ethiopia nowadays.

According to the opinions of the rulers, and political ideology, there are various kinds of federal government administrational structures. They are formed based on the Constitution of the country. If all the decentralized (federal) government administrational structures are designed in the appropriate manner, and in accordance with the Constitution, the freedom of the mass media is ensured. Then the journalists shall have their professional freedom and be beneficiaries of their rights and services.

The country will conduct its fifth parliamentary election in May 2015. Although Ethiopia is a constitutionally recognized multiparty state, the ruling party has controlled the Police and intelligence, as well as all the state institutions, including the Judiciary, Mass media, Parliament, and the Electoral Board.

As opposition to the ruling party is not tolerated, hundreds of political party leaders and their members have been imprisoned. The fates of politicians within the Oromo People's Congress (OPC), the Coalition for Unity and Democracy (CUD), the Unity for Democracy and Justice Party (UDJ), and the All Ethiopian Unity Party (AEUP) are cases in point. Nowadays, the above-mentioned political parties collapsed.

The seizure of power has been guided by force rather than by democratic means. Thus, the democratic freedom and social justice aspirations of the people have never been attained so far in Ethiopia.

ANNEXE II

Origin of Modern Mass Media in Ethiopia

The beginning of the modern media in Ethiopia traces back to different periods depending on the type of media. The following seven media channels are providing service in the country; their respective beginnings are described below.

Since Ethiopia is one of the oldest civilizations in the world, it has its own alphabet. The development of literary tradition dates back to 2000 B.C. However, modern media began to take root in the late 19th century during the reign of Emperor Menilik II who was the pioneer in introducing modernization to Ethiopia.

Newspapers

"*Awaj-Negari*" was published with news and other topics, linking the Emperor with the educated members of the society. The French also started a printing service in the Eastern city of Harar. They are mentioned by historians for their contribution to the prevention of leprosy, which was a serious disease at the time. They taught the public – through an information campaign – that leprosy was not hereditary and that it could be medically treated.

After the 1896 Battle of Adwa against Italian invaders, information was delivered to the people once a week in a handwritten newspaper prepared by Blata Gebre Egziabher. The content of the newspaper focused on national unity, integrity, and the importance of modernization. Blata Gebre Egziabher was a warrior during the Italian invasion and was imprisoned by the Italians in Nakuri Island around Massawa. He prepared the handwritten newspaper after victory upon the Emperor's order.

In 1902, the first modern newspaper *Aemro* which literally means intelligence) was printed in Addis Ababa with funding from the government. The newspaper may be taken as the first modern Amharic language newspaper in the country. The first printed copies were only fifty, which later grew to 200.

As Emperor Menelik encouraged private media at the time, small printing presses and media sprang up. In 1921 Ras Teferi Mekonen (later Emperor Hailesellassie I) started printing newspapers in Amharic and French in the Genete Leoul Palace (currently Addis Ababa University) by his "Teferi Mekonen Printing Press" .

Ras Teferri Mekonen became the first founder of private press in the country. In 1923, he brought additional printing presses from Europe, and in 1924 started a weekly newspaper called Berhannena Selam (Light and Peace). The 500 copies newspaper was edited by Gebrekristos Teklehimanot and distributed by two horsemen every Thursday. Emperor Hailesellassie donated the Palace to the Hailesellassie I University (currently Addis Ababa University). After this transfer he named his printing press Berhannena Selam. Later on, he established the largest printing press, i.e., Berhanina Selam Printing Press at Arat Kilo, which is the biggest in the country to date.

The Berhanena Selam newspaper served as a main public relations weapon for Teferi to help him to be crowned as King of Kings. Aemro served as a government press until that time along with Berhannena Selam.

Hailesellassi I ordered the publishing of different newspapers in different languages, especially after the second Italian invasion, so that he could communicate with the rest of the world. These were:

Name of newspaper	First year printed	Language
Daily News Bulletin'	1940s	French & English
Sendek Alamachin	1941	Amharic & Arabic
Addis Zemen	1941	Amharic
The Ethiopian Herald	1943	English
Yezareytu Ethiopia	1952	Amharic & French
Hibret (After the Eritrean Confederation with Ethiopia)	1961	Tigrigna & Amharic
Yezaretu Ethiopia (Again)	1965	Amharic

Radio

The first radio station was established in 1935 in Addis Ababa at the former Akaki, now Nifas Silk area. However, regular broadcasting services began in Ethiopia in 1941. The name of the station at the time was "Addis Ababa Radio" (in 1956 changed into "Ethiopian Radio").

As the Italian invasion was approaching in 1935, Ethiopian soldiers demolished the radio station to prevent the Italians from using it for their propaganda. However, the Italians repaired the broken radio station and they moved it to the current Addis Ababa University's School of Journalism and Communication. They upgraded it to a higher technical level.

After the Italian occupation ended, the radio station continued. It was the first station in Africa to broadcast services in its own language. in a sovereign state. At the time, the station was managed by the then Ministry of Pen's (the current Ministry of Education) Communication and Press department. The station started two shortwave broadcasts in French, Kiswahili, and Arabic, next to the existing Amharic, Somali, and English broadcasting service. It provided services for West and North-western Africa, Western Europe, North Africa, the Middle East and Central Africa. In 1966 an attempt was made to deliver services with good sound quality through the installation of a broadcast station in Addis Ababa, Asmara and Harar.

In 1963, a radio station named Bisrate-Wongel (the Voice of Gospel) was officially opened by the Lutheran Christian Federation providing international service from Zenebe-werek, South-West of Addis Ababa.

Radio Fana is a commercial radio station belonging to the ruling party which monopolizes radio frequencies in the country. The radio is promoting the interests of the ruling party, TPLF and is fighting against free thought in the country.

The Tigray-based *Dimtsi Woyane Radio* served as a propaganda tool for TPLF during the armed struggle. The radio is working nowadays under the cover of a commercial, but still isn't serving as an alternative source of information to *Radio Fana*.

The private-owned *Sheger* FM 102.1 is better than other radio stations in terms of popularity and acceptance. It is serving as a favorite station for many listeners, as confirmed by independent studies. The station has limited access on FM 102.1 in Addis Ababa and surrounding areas only. It is being broadcasted all over the world via the Internet. The broadcast language is Amharic which limits its reach and influence.

Afro FM is the only private FM station serving as a station for foreigners residing in Addis Ababa. It is broadcasting in English and French. Considering the behaviour of the ruling party, it is not expected that the radio station can be fully independent.

Television
The first Ethiopian Television broadcast service also launched on 25 April 1964. The official broadcasting of the television began on 2 November 1964. The installations of the station were built at Addis Ababa's new city hall, during the time that the organization of African Unity was established in Addis Ababa.

Mass Media during the Post-1974 Revolution Period
Except for a change in content, there were no significant changes in the media during the Derg regime (1974-1991). *Bisrate-Wongel Radio Station* was taken over by government in 1977, and re-named *Ethiopian Revolutionary Radio*. Still, national and international broadcasts services were being aired.

The main governmental newspapers at the time were *Addis Zemen*, *Ethiopian Herald* (10,000 copies), Berissa (*Oromiffa*) (14,000 copies), and *Al-alem* (in Arabic). A magazine called *Zemen* also published by the Ethiopian News Agency at the time.

New newspapers were started during this time; especially the *Serto Ader* newspaper was started in 1979 by the ruling party. Its circulation was 200,000 copies. This newspaper was the Marxist-Leninist mouthpiece for the government. Its distribution was targeted at party's rank and file. The *Revolutionary Police* newspaper (started in 1976) had a distribution of up to 100,000 copies. Similarly, the army newspaper *Tatek* was distributed to army staff up to 28,000 copies. Another party organ was *Meskerem*, reflecting Marxist-Leninist ideology; its distribution was 117,000 copies. There was also the *Voice of Ethiopia* newspaper which was published from 1958 to1968 by the Ethiopian Patriots Association, as well as English and Amharic magazines called *Addis Reporter*, and *Mennen*.

The *Dergue* banned private presses in a proclamation; neither did the 1987 Constitution allow the existence of private media, except state media and party organs. Every other publication was censored.

The radio broadcast services from abroad included the Voice of America's (VOA) Amharic, Oromiffa and Tigrigna service, and Radio Deutsche Welle (Germany). There was also a private English language newspaper *The Daily Monitor*.

_ Overview of mass media since the 1990s [8]

Print Media

The 1991 Transitional Charter introduced by the EPRDF allowed freedom of expression and press for the first time in Ethiopia's history. In addition, the 1995 Constitution – as well as the Press Proclamation – guaranteed the right to freedom of expression and press. A good many private newspapers sprang up until the 2005 elections when the regime shut down most of the private newspapers.[9] Meanwhile, the state media including radio, television and newspapers, had continued to serve the political interests of the regime, despite the fact that the Transitional Charter envisioned them to serve the public with impartiality.

There was one private newspaper called *Eyeta* in 1992. After 1992 more than private 630 newspapers and 130 magazines were licensed. Four magazines and newspapers were printed by the government, four by political parties, eight by religious institutions, and the remainder by private owners *Tomar*, *Tobiya*, *Menilik*, *Reporter*, *Nation*, *Addis Zena* and *Addis Admas* and were among the leading Amharic weekly newspapers at that time.

Most of the private newspapers went out of market after the 2005 election. Editors and journalists of most newspapers were imprisoned, while others

8 A description of the origin of modern mass media in Ethiopia is included in Annexe I.
9 As per the study of Population Media Center (2006) there were approximately 80 presses printing between 1991 and 2005.

were forced to leave the country. As a result, the hope of a thriving free press in Ethiopia was dashed. In 2012 the private independent press in Ethiopia amounted to 40, i.e., 16 newspapers (11 Amharic and 5 English) and 24 magazines (1 Amharic-English, 21 Amharic and 2 in English). In December 2014 their numbers had dropped to 27 due to mass imprisonment, threats, unlawful closure of presses, and exile of journalists.

Radio and Television
For a long time, the government refused to give permission for private radio and television broadcasting. FM *Addis* 97.1 started service in 2003, which in 2014 evolved – including TV – into the Ethiopian Broadcasting Corporation. Although it was established to be accountable, The House of People's Representatives, decided that the TV's editorial policy (including all programs) would fall under the strict control of the Government's Communication Affairs Office, so as to serve the ruling party's interest. An alternative television station, Ethiopian Satellite Television was launched in Europe and America in April 2010, allegedly by opposition groups in the diaspora. This TV Station broadcasts anti-government information.
The government owns various radio and television channels including *Ethiopian Radio*, the *Ethiopian Broadcasting Corporation*, and eight regional stations belonging to regional states.
Besides broadcasting, the above mass communication agencies publish newspapers funded by the regional governments under close supervision of the same.

Comparison of a Media Sample in Few African Countries in August 2014

Country	Population in million	Government radio / FM	Private radio / FM	Government TV	Private TV	Print Media
Kenya	45	1	104	1	4	102
Ethiopia	94.1	20	7	1	0	50
Ghana	25	2	19	1	10	135
South Africa	48	4	358	4	552	117
Botswana	2	2	3	1	3	15

Source: each country's internet data and official of the countries concerned (2014).

All print media in Kenya are in private hands; Ghana, Botswana and South Africa each have one government broadcast media; the remaining ones belong to the private sector. From the 50 press results in Ethiopia, 23 are administered and supervised by the government. From among the 13 newspapers under government's supervision 1 is in English, 1 in Arabic, 2 in Oromiffa, 1 in Somali, 1 in Tigrigna, and 7 in Amharic. They are printed and distributed throughout the country through the government structure. Similarly, from among the 10 magazines under government supervision, 1 is in English, 1 in Somali, 1 in Tigrigna, 1 in Afar, and 6 in Amharic.

News Agencies and Broadcast Media

There are two large news agencies, i.e., the government-owned *Ethiopian News Agency* (ENA) and *Walta Information Center* (owned by the ruling party, TPLF). The main objective of these agencies is to collect local news from reliable sources, including the international media, and sell the same to national and international clients. ENA broadcasts 300 news items per day on the web. The agency used to operate with some autonomy until it fell under the government's Communication Affairs Office after the 2005 election.

Walta Information Center was established by the ruling party. It broadcasts and releases distorted information in times of political, social and economic grievances against the government. Their programs and documentaries all favour the ruling party's interests. *Walta* accomplishes different tasks. In addition to serving as news agency, it facilitates discussions with the support of different governmental and non-governmental bodies, as well as educational meetings and business exhibitions. It also prepares news pages and releases several documentaries and serves as source of information for the West regarding Ethiopia and East Africa.

Community Radio and Commercial Radio

Community radio is supposed to be a non-profit radio service established by the community to serve as alternative channels for the community. These radio stations are only accountable to their community and they serve as alternative information channel without any influence from the government. However, in Ethiopia community radios are government-funded. Thus, they have no use other than reflecting the voice of the ruling party. There are 17 community radio station fully funded by different departments of government and seven commercial broadcasting radio stations in Ethiopia.

As already noted, there are also several international broadcast media outlets including *VOA Radio* in Amharic, Oromiffa and Tigrigna from the USA, *Radio Deutsche-Welle* in Amharic from Germany, Vatican Radio from Vatican City, ESAT Radio and Television from the USA, England and the Netherlands, Oromia media Network (OMN) from the USA, Berekah Broadcasting Network, BBN radio from USA and Ethiopian Broadcasting Service (EBS) Television from the USA. In addition, there are also many radio stations transmitting from different regions of Africa, the USA, Australia, and Europe who serve the Ethiopian audience in different local languages, focusing on political, social, and religious issues.

Although their content and mode of presentation differs from one to the other, they typically focus on social, political, economic, and religious matters. All channels, except have limited air time, yet they serve as alternative sources of information. provides a 24/7 service and serves as alternative source of information for Ethiopians living abroad as well as in the country.

The VOA and Deutsche-Welle radios are often jammed by the ruling party, especially during elections or during more sensitive political problems. The costs involved in blocking both orbital and terrestrial transmissions, either specifically or in general, and jamming wave and internet broadcasting, vary between $50,000 and $500 million, which constitutes a heavy loss of tax payers money.

Telecommunications

For information freedom, least cost, quality and accessible services, there need to be telecommunication services, affordable and free from censorship. Government should create the conditions for affordable and a censor-free telecommunication service. However, in Ethiopia telecommunications is under total control of government and limits the right of freedom to information. Every telecommunication service, especyially the phone communication, is completely controlled by the government's Information Network Security Agency (INSA). Moreover, it is costly and of low quality. The table below shows Ethiopia's poor telecommunication service provision compared to other African countries.

Telecommunication Service Accessibility in Some of African Countries in 2013

Country	Population in millions	Under government	Private owned provider	Landline access in 100%	Mobile phone access in 100%	Internet penetration in 100%
Algeria	39.2	01	29	8.1	73	16.5
Libya	6.2	01	04	12.6	148	16.5
South Africa	52.9	01	34	7.8	151	48.9
Zimbabwe	14.1	01	17	2	114	18.5
Ethiopia	94.1	01	0	1	11.5	1.9
Kenya	44.3	*0	04	1.3	74.4	39
Nigeria	173.6	02	10	1.4	96.8	38
Ghana	25.9	01	24	1.2	112	12.3

*Sources: World Bank, ITU, and African Telecommunication usage stats (2014).

*Ethiopia data shows below 2% penetration rate of the internet and landline accessibility compared with comparable African countries. Also the mobile phone accessibility is very low compared with other African countries; its penetration rate is below 2 %.

ANNEXE III

Large Scale Land Allocations and Rent Prices

Region	Tigray	Afar	Amhara	Oromia	SNNPR	Gambella	Benishangul-gumuz	Ethiopian-Somali
Allocated land in ha.	51,544	409,678	420,000	1,057,866	348,009	829,199	691,984	26,000
Partial data of land Transferred to investors in ha.	X	54,000	121,370	380,000	60,500	535,000	191,500	X
Price rent per year/per ha. (ETB)	30-40	X	14-79	70-135	30-117	20-30	15-25	16-65

*Source: Desalegn Rahmato (2011) and International institute for Environment and Development (2014).

X- The data not confirmed by author.

*The above data shows only the large land allocated and transferred to private investors; not included are the 335,000 hectare huge state investments for the Kuraz Sugar Project of Southern Lower Omo, the Grand Renaissance Dam of Benishangul-Guz, Gil Gebi I, II & III dam projects, the Illubabor Fertilizer Industry, the Welkite-tegedie and Kesem Sugar Projects, and the like.

ANNEXE IV

Basic Principles of Journalism

Truthfulness and Credible: A journalist has the responsibility to gather, assess, cross-check and distribute correct and credible information based on the values of society, and by ensuring whether the information is relevant for the interest of society in general and the target audience in particular. The journalist also forwards recommendations and remedies to be implemented by government and other stakeholders in pursuit of a society's well-being.

Balance: A journalist should be loyal to the need of society and stick to the principle of truthfulness. This requires the journalist to refrain from expressing personal views in favour or against any interest groups. The journalist should also facilitate presenting various views rather than presenting biased content. When interest groups are not willing to comment on controversial issues, their names and their position and address should be disclosed.

Accountability: Each and every journalist is expected to avoid mistakes at all times, because any mistake may lead to unforeseen consequences for the society. Therefore, journalists are advised to crosscheck the information from different sources before presenting it to the audience. If any journalist commits wrongdoing, he/she will be liable to administrative as well as legal measures.

Free and Impartial: First, the journalist should be free from personal biases and prejudice regarding political, religious, and other issues. The only way to avoid a guilty conscience and legal liability is by doing his/her work based on these principles. The focus of the journalist should be on assessing the correctness and the credibility of the information.

Obeying the Principles of the Profession: The journalist is to ensure the proper utilization of resources, including air time, office space and equipment. Journalists are to investigate issues that serve the interest of society, and to unravel wrongdoings committed by different groups. Journalists should refrain from exaggerating issues and from skipping relevant information.

Competence: The journalist is expected to prepare himself/herself for the duties of the profession. One of the means to ensure this is by a proper selection of words and terminologies, by prior assessment of the potential consequences of the information, and its effect on the target audience. The journalist should upgrade his skills and knowledge, adapt modern technologies, and strive to be influential in a positive way.

Professional integrity: The journalist is to assess the relevance and correctness of the information before presenting it to the audience. The journalist should be aware of the editorial policy of the media and he/she should obey the regulations. The journalist should have awareness and a clear understanding of the laws of the land and the values of the society as well as its culture. The journalist never compromises the ethics and principles of the profession at any time and place, so as to maintain professional integrity.

_ References

አለቃ ታዬ (1924)፦**የኢትዮጵያ ሀዝብ ታሪክ**፦ሚሲኦንግ ሱኤድዋ ማተሚያ፦ አስመራ

ተክለ ጻድቅ መኩሪያ(1965)፦**የኢትዮጵያ ታሪክ**፦ ኑብያ (ናፓታ-መርዌ)፦ ብርሃንና ሰላም፦አዲስ አበባ

ላጺሶ ጊ.ዼሌቦ (1982)፦**የኢትዮጵያ ሬጅም የህዝብና የመንግስት ታሪክ**፦አዲስ አበባ

ገስጥ ተጫኔ/ ዘነብ ፌለቀ (1996) ፦ **ነቢር** ንግድ ማተሚያ ድርጅት፦ አዲስ አበባ

ባህሩ ዘውዴ (1999) ፦**የኢትዮጵያ ታሪክ**፦ከ1847 እስከ 1983 ዓ.ም.፦ አዲስ አበባ ዩኒቨርስቲ ፕሬስ፦ አዲስ አበባ

የኢትዮጵያ ብሮድካስት ባለስጣን (2003) ፦**መገናኛ ብዙኃን**፦**ዓመታዊ መፅሔት** ፦ አዲስ አበባ ኢትዮጵያ

ዳንኤል ተፈራ (2003) ፦ **ዳንዲ**፦ **የነጋሶ መንገድ**፦ ንግድ ማተሚያ ድርጅት፦ አዲስ አበባ

ኮሎኔል መንግስቱ ኃይለማርያም (2004)፦**ትግላችን**፦ **የኢትዮጵያ ሕዝብ አብዮታዊ የትግል ታሪክ**፦ቅጽ 1፦ፀሐይ አሳታሚ፦ ካሊፎርኒያ፦ አሜሪካ

ዶ/ር መረራ ጉዲና (2005)፦የኢትዮጵያ ፖለቲካ ምስቅልቅል ጉዞ እና የህይወቴ ትዝታዎች፦ከኢትዮጵያ ተማሪዎች ንቅናቄ እስከ ኢህአዴግ፦ ግራፊክስ ፕሪንተርስ፦አዲስ አበባ

Federal Negarit Gazeta (1995), **Federal Democratic Republic of Ethiopia Constitution 'proclamation' no. 1/1995**, Berehannena Selam Printing Enterprise, Addis Ababa.

Feederal Negarit Gazeta (2007), Broadcasting services proclamation no. **533/2007**: Berehannena Selam Printing Enterprise, Addis Ababa.

Federal Negarit Gazeta (2008) ፦ **Freedom of the mass media and access to information proclamation no. 590/2008**, Berehannena Selam Printing Enterprise, Addis Ababa.

Federal Negarit Gazeta (2009), **Anti-terrorism proclamation no.652/2009**, Berhannena Selam Printing Enterprise, Addis Ababa.

Negussie Tefera (1988), **The Role of Mass Communication in Social and**

64

Economic Development in Some Developing Countries and the Case of Ethiopia, University of Wales, Cardiff UK.

Pankhurst, R. (1998), **The Ethiopians, A History**. Malden: Blackwell Publishers, Inc.

Woo-Cumings, M. (1999). **The Developmental State**. Cornell University Press.

Chang, Ha-Joon.(1999) **"The Economic Theory of the Developmental State."** Pp. 182-199 in Woo-Cumings, M. (ed.), **The Developmental State**. Ithaca, NY: Cornall University Press.

International IDEA Handbook Series 4(2001), **Democracy at the Local Level,** Bulls Tryckeri, Halmstad, Sweden.

Myrdal, G. (2001), **Against the Sream: Critical Essays on Economics**; the Journal of Economic Issues; New York, USA.

Afr.j.polit. sci. (2002), **Ethnic Federalism, Fiscal Reform, Development and Democracy,** Vol 7 No. 1.

Gudina, M. (2002) '**Ethiopia: Competing Ethnic Nationalisms and the Quest for Democracy**, 1960-2000', ISS, The Hague, The Netherlands.

Willis, K. (2005), **Theories and Practices of Development**. London: Routledge.

Nafzier, E.W. (2006),**The meaning of economic development**, United Nation University ;Research No. 20.

World Bank. (2006), **World Development Report 2007-Development and the Next Generation**. New York: Oxford University Press for the World Bank.

Population Media Center (2006), **Ethiopian Mass Media Profile**, Addis Ababa University, Addis Ababa, Ethiopia.

African Union (2007), **African Charter on Democracy, Elections, and Governance;** Addis Ababa, Ethiopia.

Flint, C. & Taylor, P. (2007). **Political Geography: World Economy, Nation-State, and Locality** (5th ed.). Pearson/Prentice Hall.

Ng, C. (2008), **The 'Developmental State' and Economic Development,** Oxford University; http://www.e-ir.info/2008/06/15/the-developmental-state-and-economic-development/

Harcup, T. (2009), **Journalism: Principles and Practice**, Thousand Oaks, California: Sage Publications, ISBN 978-1847872500, OCLC 280437077.

International Crisis Group (2009), **Ethiopian: Ethnic Federalism and its Content;** African report No. 153.

Dessalegn, R. (2011), **LAND TO INVESTORS: Large-Scale Land Transfers in Ethiopia,** Forum for Social Studies, Addis Ababa.

Lerch, H. (2011), **An introduction to Political Philosophy**, www.HubertLerch.com ISBN-13: 978-1468056068.

Cilliers, J., et,al (2011), **African Future 2050**, Central Printing press, Addis Ababa, Ethiopia.

Skjerdal, T. (2011): **Development Journalism Revived: the Case of Ethiopia;** 74(2011).http://www.tandfonline.com/doi/abs

Uttara, M. (2011) **"Different Types of Mass Media".** Buzzle.com.

Alemayehu, T. (2013), **Social Media as an Alternative Political Forum in Ethiopia: The Case of Facebook,** Addis Ababa University, Addis Ababa (Unpublished).

Olana, B. (2014), **Pride versus Humility:** The Self-Perceived Paradoxical Identities of Ethiopian Journalists; http://sgo.sagepub.com/content/4/1/2158244014528921

Frances Thomson (2014), **WHY WE NEED THE CONCEPT OF LAND-GRAB-INDUCED DISPLACEMENT**, University of Sussex, England http://journalinternaldisplacement.webs.com/submission.htm

Keeley, J., et.al, (2014), **Large-scale land deals in Ethiopia: Scale, trends, features and outcomes to date**, IIED.

https://cpj.org/blog/2014/12/mission-journal-in-ethiopia-journalists-must-choos.php#more

http://www.hrw.org/reports/2015/01/20/journalism-not-crime
The Universal Declaration of Human Rights, http://www.un.org/en/documents/udhr

http://www.itu.int/en/Pages/default.aspx Africa - Fixed-line, Internet and Broadband Statistics

http://www.internetsociety.org/map/global-internet-report

http://www.independent.co.uk/news/world/africa/ethiopia-forcing-out-thousands-in-land-grab-6291029.html

http://www.internetworldstats.com/africa.htm

http://www.solidaritymovement.org/downloads/120618-HRWs-New-Report-Confirms-Land http://www.hrw.org/sites/default/files/reports/ethiopia0612webwcover_0.pdf-Grabs.pdf

http://www.ophi.org.uk/wp-content/uploads/Ethiopia-2013.pdf?79d83
ITU Africa - Mobile Voice and Data Communications Statistics

IFJ (International Federation of Journalists) - **Declaration of Principles on the Conduct of Journalists** (DOC version)

SPJ (Society of Professional Journalists) - **Code of Ethics**